New Hampshire's Political
TROUBADOUR

A Guide to the Year 2000
First-in-the-Nation Presidential Primary

PRESENTING

FOR THE FIRST TIME ANYWHERE

AN ALPHABETICAL APPENDIX LISTING EVERY CANDIDATE

WHO HAS EVER RUN IN A NEW HAMPSHIRE PRESIDENTIAL PRIMARY

1952 ~ 1996

INCLUDING NAME, PARTY AFFILIATION, ELECTION YEAR/S & VOTES RECEIVED

Resources of New Hampshire, Inc. February, 1999

41123236

Printed on 70# Astrolite Smooth Text - Monadnock Mills, Inc., Bennington, NH

Printing: Puritan Press, Inc., Hollis, NH

Design: Todd Smith / Design, Penacook, NH

Published by: Resources of New Hampshire, Inc., Nashua, NH

Limited edition

ISBN 0-9637615-2-8

Library of Congress Catalog Card Number: 98-68671

NEW HAMPSHIRE'S POLITICAL TROUBADOUR

Why A Troubadour?

IN THE SPRING OF 1931 Don Tuttle, the Executive Secretary of New Hampshire's Department of Publicity, introduced the NEW HAMPSHIRE TROUBADOUR, a monthly publication "singing the praises of New Hampshire."

It recounted "New Hampshire folks, their ideals, their ways, their standards, their hopes, their accomplishments, their adventures in neighborliness." Its lifespan lasted twenty years.

NEW HAMPSHIRE'S POLITICAL TROUBADOUR is an inheritance specifically dedicated to the tradition of the country's first-in-the-nation presidential preference primary and the rich political heritage upon which it is founded. Wherever appropriate, this progeny quotes freely from its ancestor.

You'll find here the fabric of the political folklife unique to the Granite State.

THE NATION'S FIRST VOTER

Neil Tillotson is referred to as "The Wizard of Dixville Notch" by New England Business magazine. Their appellation does not begin to identify this eminent man who is New Hampshire's quintessential Horatio Alger. Though born across the river in Vermont, we claim him as one of our own. Humble and self-effacing, the self-styled "kid from Beecher Falls" has built and operated international businesses, becoming one of New Hampshire's most successful and revered entrepreneurs. He is a stalwart supporter of the North Country, with the same granite strength as the Old Man of the Mountains.

From the myriad of his achievements, there's one priceless record no one else will ever cap:

Neil Tillotson, Moderator of Dixville, has cast the first vote in the nation in every general election for President beginning in 1964.

At 100 years of age in 1998, this remarkable Granite State citizen anticipates adding to his quadrennial record in the year 2000 by being the first voter in the new millennium to cast his ballot for President of the United States.

Troubadour January, 1932

In your own pine grove you'll find an ax a splendid substitute for a golf club.

THE SECOND-GREATEST SHOW ON EARTH

It's midwinter when the decisive day comes. Though the bears sleep in the invigorating climate, the rest of us relax, just as comfortably, in the heat of the presidential cauldron and the hot air of those who stir it. For all of its significance, it's like a day at the circus when the tumblers, clowns, barkers, acrobats and high-flyers come to town to entertain us.

We're not even disturbed that cotton candy and popcorn are overpriced, because we know the actors live on sugar and corn. What do we care if they think we're country bumpkins? Doesn't every newspaper, radio station and TV network in the nation broadcast to the world about our state?

What we enjoy most is the early arrival of the donkeys who haul the canvas and the elephants who pull up the tent poles. During the weeks it takes them to set up the extravaganza in our pasture they are right at home with the old bull.

If you believe only one half of what their handlers tell you, you're smart. If you know which half, you're brilliant. But everybody has a good time and gets their full money's worth. And as Lady Godiva rides sidesaddle around the ring, the candidates' men on each side yell, "Hurray for our side!"

Most of the jockeys in our horse race nobody will remember when it's all over. We've had Robert Kelleher who probably thought he was running for Prime Minister because his platform was to replace Congress with Parliament. Who recalls poet "Roll-in

Robinson," alleged grandson of Crazy Horse, with his wife, the "Magic Princess?" Or Roger Durrett, running around the state in a white suit hoping he'd be mistaken for Mark Twain? So costumed,

Troubadour April, 1936

Story told by Winthrop L. Carter of Nashua, President of the New England Council, speaking before the famous Gresham Club of London, England.

A travelling salesman for a spray chemical concern arrived early one morning at Hollis Depot on a trip from New York. He found himself at a little railroad station located in the woods, without a house in sight. He turned to the station agent and said, "Where is the town?" The agent replied, "About four miles up the hill." He said, "How do you get up there? Have you any taxis?" The agent said, "No, but the Deacon most generally comes down to fetch the mail and like as not he will give you a ride." Just then the Deacon appeared and the drummer asked him for a ride. The Deacon replied, "Certain. Get right in and we'll get going just as soon as I get the mail." As they started away from the station the drummer turned to the Deacon and said, "I call this a devil of a note, to dump a man off here in the wood. Why don't they have the station up in the town?" "Well, now, that's an idea," said the Deacon, "you'd have the depot right up in the village?" "Sure," said the drummer, "that's where it belongs." "Well, mebbe so," says the Deacon, "but of course some folks thinks it's handier to have it down by the railway."

he was more likely to have been reclaimed as a state hospital escapee.

Jack Mabardy wanted the government to devise a training course to prevent a possible takeover by UFOs. Princess Runningwaters arrived decked out in animal skins. "Love 22" handed out $22 dollar bills with his Uncle Sam likeness centered on the currency as if he were Thomas Jefferson. Vermin Supreme wore a boot on his head and carried a giant toothbrush as "the friendly fascist, a tyrant you can trust."

Unfortunately, some had bad luck. With a theme, "To make America a safe place to live," Robert Haines ended up in the slammer for brandishing a rifle while wearing a bullet proof vest. Dressed as Uncle Sam, Sam Rouseville was driving a Japanese car when he was nabbed for speeding in his haste to file at Concord. Then there was our native son, Lyndon LaRouche, who spent five years in the federal pen for mail fraud and conspiracy, and Irwin Schiff, jailed for three years as a "political prisoner" for not paying his income tax.

All of these forgettable candidates are like Fred Allen's horse who never won any races, but he was always the happiest horse in the race because Fred gave him eight mint juleps in the paddock.

As long as we continue our omniscience in predicting the choice of the nation's presidents, as we've done for the past nearly half century, maybe presidential elections should not only begin in New Hampshire, but should also end here. It would save the candidates, the media and the taxpayers bundles of dough and evade lots of hassle. We could then do P.T. Barnum one better by staging an even greater show. And admission would be free, in Granite State tradition.

The Most Unusual Primary Candidate?

Over the past two decades, New Hampshire Secretary of State Bill Gardner has met some unusual presidential candidates. In fact, one of them wasn't even human! As a publicity stunt, the owners of Benson's Wild Animal Farm in Hudson attempted to sign up their resident gorilla, Colossus, as a primary candidate. Because the great ape couldn't fit into a car, handlers drove a chimpanzee to Concord to stand in for him. But Secretary Gardner ruled against the filing because Colossus didn't meet federal age requirements. He was only 16 years old.

THE FIRST PRESIDENTIAL PRIMARIES—
WHY NEW HAMPSHIRE?

I t's partly tradition. From 1920, they've been held here first. In those early days we used to elect delegates who made our presidential selection.

Since 1952, we've balloted directly for the presidential candidate of our choice. What's more, except for a technical aberration in 1992, when Democrats supported our neighbor from Massachusetts, we've always voted "Always First, Always Right."

It's a waste of money for other states to hold subsequent caucuses or primaries, or even the national party conventions, since the Granite State election has previously identified the next president.

Jealous of the infallibility of our state's track record, now everyone wants to muscle in on our first-in-the-nation primary. Big states California and New York have moved their primaries up closer. Even smaller states like Delaware are licking their chops for a bite of the pie. For them, peace in presidential politics is spelled "piece."

Because we set the pace, "frontloading" has become a new word in the lexicon of presidential politics. Our citizens welcome all presidential wannabees — over 100 of them competed in the last two elections.

It takes millions of dollars to run for the presidency elsewhere, but not up here. For example, the evangelical afflatus, "Messiah," limited his expense to printing business cards. Unfortunately in his case, though he spread his message widely and inexpensively, he didn't show.

Candidates don't have to be independently wealthy or raise money from special interest groups to qualify. If they do well here, money comes pouring in. If they fail here, no matter how much dough they use, they're broke. Still, all the players get the chance for a head start with media hype.

To win, the high-rollers must take off their black business suits, get out of their limos, start shaking hands and act like they love the place. It isn't hard, because our citizens revere this day in history when New Hampshire becomes the nation's most significant address. Sure, the foreigners may have to put up with snowy and blustery weather, but where else can they get better photo ops than here — milking cows in a freezing barn or sledding with unrestrained four-year-olds?

Perhaps we've been too smug in our tradition as the home of presidential primary politics. Nonetheless it's a logical prerogative, considering that the Republican Party was founded in Exeter on October 12, 1853. Fortunately, it has taken other states a long time to wise up to our quadrennial blessing.

As The Old Man of the Mountains summed it up, "We got'ta good thing go'in up he'ya and ain't go'in to give it up."

Troubadour July, 1945

The first public library in America was the Dublin Juvenile Library, established in 1822. It was supported by voluntary contribution but the use of it was free to all.

RICHARD UPTON MAKES CHANGE

The presidential primary has been held in New Hampshire since 1916, and it has been first-in-the-nation since 1920. But the state's role in selecting future presidents did not emerge until 1952. That year, New Hampshire voters for the first time selected candidates themselves, not just delegates pledged to specific candidates. Richard Upton of Concord, Speaker of the New Hampshire House of Representatives, introduced legislation in 1949 that changed the nature of the New Hampshire primary by electing the party standard bearers rather than their delegates. His goal was to make the primary more interesting and meaningful. Its achievement made the New Hampshire primary a critical stop on the road to the White House for all serious presidential aspirants and made the first-in-the-nation primary the premiere political event in America.

1952: The Democratic Primary

Incumbent President Harry S. Truman called the New Hampshire primary "eyewash," saying that he wouldn't run because he already owned the nomination. He reversed himself after five days of bad publicity, but never visited the state. After his stunning loss here, Truman withdrew from the race. His victorious primary opponent, meanwhile, established a New Hampshire tradition. Tennessee Senator Estes Kefauver campaigned tirelessly, bypassing party bigwigs for direct local support. His popular one-on-one style set the high standard for grassroots campaigning that New Hampshire voters still expect from primary candidates today.

NH POLITICAL PROFILE:
"BIG JOHN" PILLSBURY

John Pillsbury of Manchester was a giant of a man in both physical stature and brilliant intellect. A thunderous orator. A one-time majority Republican leader of the state legislature. Whenever he was at the podium, the gallery overflowed. Perhaps he was the best spellbinder from New Hampshire since Daniel Webster. Webster was his vicarious mentor, and Dan would have been proud of John. A bust of Webster occupied a place of honor just inside John's front door where visitors were expected to give it due reverence as they entered.

Thanks to his quick wit, mischievous good humor and practical jokes, John always had the last word. When General Douglas MacArthur was retired from military service and came to New Hampshire for his last public appearance, the General addressed a crowd of 2,500 at the state Armory for a "fun dinner" in his honor.

Troubadour September, 1945

Daniel Webster once said, "Men hang out their signs indicative of their respective trades: shoe makers hang out a gigantic shoe; jewelers a monster watch, and the dentist hangs out a gold tooth; but up in the mountains of New Hampshire, God Almighty has hung out a sign to show that there He makes men."

Henry Long, Massachusetts Liquor Revenue Commissioner, had been invited as a special guest because his minions had been taking license plate numbers of Massachusetts residents who purchased liquor from New Hampshire stores. As they crossed the border en route home, they would be grabbed by Massachusetts police to pay the Bay State tax. John, unannounced, walked up to the head table and presented Long with a ten-gallon bottle of scotch in appreciation for his attendance.

Pillsbury was as talented a writer as he was a speaker. In Washington he served and wrote speeches for Senators Styles Bridges and Robert Taft. In New Hampshire he was a member of Governor Sherman Adams' "Kitchen Cabinet." Because he had been a reporter for Bill Loeb's *Manchester Union Leader*, he displayed both political principle and courage in working for Adams, who supported both General Eisenhower for President and a sales tax,

---

Troubadour August, 1931

A bronze tablet recently placed on the Squamscott Hotel, Exeter, NH, reads, "On this site The Republican Party was first so named by Hon. Amos Tuck, October 12, 1853." As a great leader Amos Tuck conferred lasting distinction on the State of New Hampshire in the history of the nation, by being the earliest champion in the cause of human freedom, and by giving the name "Republican" to the forces gathered to resist slavery. An informal meeting was held at Major Blake's Hotel (now the Squamscott Hotel) on October 12, 1853, and Mr. Tuck suggested the name "Republican" to be given to the new party. This was several months before the mass meeting at Ripon, Wisconsin, at which the same name was adopted.

1952: The Republican Primary

After twenty years of Democratic rule in the White House, the Republican Party hoped to provide a candidate who would inspire voters to switch. New Hampshire Governor Sherman Adams spearheaded the effort to persuade General Dwight D. Eisenhower, the hero of D-Day, to run as a Republican. Eisenhower, still serving as Supreme Commander of NATO forces, was prohibited from campaigning for the nomination, and never came to New Hampshire. Nevertheless, he easily defeated Ohio Senator Robert Taft in the first so-called "beauty contest" primary, and went on to serve two terms as President.

two constant targets of Loeb's rancor.

A graduate of the Harvard Divinity School, Pillsbury served in the Pacific with the rank of Navy Chaplain during World War II. He'd take his officer allotment of beer and share the privilege in religious discussions with enlisted men who had no such perk. Though not known to have had a parish of his own in the Granite State, he delivered a classic eulogy for a friend, Reubin Moore. Reub was the legendary New Hampshire Yankee farmer in appearance, demeanor and locution. Those who heard Pillsbury's fire and brimstone speech say it was so effective that some of the good citizens of Bradford feared lest it'd bring Reub back.

While studying at Amherst College, John was a student of poet Robert Frost. Their relationship evolved into a lifelong friendship. At Frost's request, John Pillsbury was the catalyst for the state's acquisition of the poet's birthplace in Derry, an invaluable addition to its historic sites. This is undoubtedly the most treasured of Big John Pillsbury's many unique legacies.

WINNERS OF NEW HAMPSHIRE PRESIDENTIAL PRIMARIES FROM 1952-1996

YEAR	REPUBLICAN	DEMOCRAT
1952	Dwight D. Eisenhower	Estes Kefauver
1956	Dwight D. Eisenhower	Estes Kefauver
1960	Richard M. Nixon	John F. Kennedy
1964	Henry Cabot Lodge	Lyndon B. Johnson
1968	Richard M. Nixon	Lyndon B. Johnson
1972	Richard M. Nixon	Edmund S. Muskie
1976	Gerald R. Ford	Jimmy Carter
1980	Ronald W. Reagan	Jimmy Carter
1984	Ronald W. Reagan	Gary Hart
1988	George H. W. Bush	Michael Dukakis
1992	George H. W. Bush	Paul Tsongas
1996	Patrick J. Buchanan	William J. Clinton

WHAT PRICE THE PRIMARY?

A study of "The Impact of New Hampshire's First-in-the-Nation Presidential Primary on the State's Economy" has been commissioned by the Political Library. In 1996 the state's Department of Economic Development estimated the event enhanced the state's overall economy by approximately $32 million, but its figures were based on information received from a limited number of sources. This study will be the first in-depth study ever undertaken to determine the primary's financial, promotional and credibility value to the state. The election "cycle" from November, 1994 to November, 1998 will be documented. The final report will be completed in 1999.

An outstanding group of talented individuals, specifically qualified to conduct the research, are undertaking the examination. It is under the leadership of Dr. Ross Gitell of the Whittemore School of Business at the University of New Hampshire. Norman

---

Troubadour January, 1937

Shortly after Christmas last year a five-year-old boy suddenly burst into flames of sulphuric blasphemy. Aghast, his mother asked him where in the world he had ever heard such language. "From Santa Claus," he replied, "he tripped over a chair in my room the night before Christmas."

Sedgley, a Whittemore School doctoral candidate, will work with Gitell on economic modeling, data collection and analysis.

Katie Paine and the Delahaye Group will record the number of visits by the media, campaigns and interest groups related to the primary to include expenditures per visit/per day and an analysis of media content. Brian Gottlieb of the New Hampshire Business and Industry Association will assist Professor Gitell on economic impact analysis, surveys, focus groups and data collection. Dr. Larry Goss of Northern Economic Planners will provide historical data on rooms and meals taxes. Senior staff members of the New Hampshire Department of Economic Development will contribute statistics on tourism and business recruitment.

The report will include documentation on the national benefits from New Hampshire's first-in-the-nation primary. It will demonstrate that New Hampshire is relatively inexpensive, thus stimulating greater candidate and voter participation while receiving international media coverage of the country's electoral process.

Troubadour December, 1939

An attempt was being made to rush a vote through town meeting in one of the small New England towns. One voter objected. The moderator demanded to know whether he was a voter in the town. He said he was. How long had he been in town? Was he a year-round resident or a summer resident? He said that he was a year-round resident and had been there for seventeen years. "Sit down," yelled the moderator. "We don't propose to have no tourist telling us what to do in this town."

PRECEDENTS SET IN NEW HAMPSHIRE PRESIDENTIAL PRIMARIES

Richard E. Nixon holds the record for having won the most New Hampshire presidential primaries; three, in 1960, 1968, 1972. When he ran for president in 1960 only fifteen other states and the District of Columbia had primaries.

No incumbent president running for re-election and who had no significant opposition on the party's New Hampshire primary ballot has ever been defeated for a second term as President: Dwight D. Eisenhower in 1956; Lyndon Baines Johnson in 1964; Richard E. Nixon in 1972; Ronald Reagan in 1984; Bill Clinton in 1996.

Although several women have participated in the presidential primaries, no woman of national stature has ever filed. Lenora B. Fulani, running as a Democrat in 1992, qualified for $642,497 in federal matching funds, yet only received 402 Democratic votes.

Former Minnesota Governor Harold E. Stassen is the honorary grandfather of the New Hampshire presidential elections, having been on the ballot seven times, beginning in 1948 with a pledged delegate who didn't win. (See page 65.)

Resulting from their primary campaign chairmanships two sitting New Hampshire governors, Sherman Adams and John H. Sununu, were appointed Chiefs of Staff to the President at the White House.

New Hampshire — Always First, Always Right

I n 1952 New Hampshire held the first of its novel presidential primaries pursuant to legislation drafted by Richard F. Upton. From our experience of the past twelve primaries, the procedures may have changed somewhat, but his original concept of our first-in-the-nation contest has withstood both time and challenge.

New Hampshire is nationally recognized as "where it all begins" in presidential elections. And well it should be, because except for one excusable exception, without winning here no candidate has ever made it to the White House.

Every four years the state gets a fresh diagnosis from the political pundits trying to psychoanalyse us. Some say there aren't enough of us for a fair sample, others say we all speak in the same Yankee twang which nobody understands. The consensus is that our folkways defy description.

Troubadour April, 1940

Learning that a "newcomer" who had lived in the town only ten years was planning to run for the Board of Selectmen, an old-timer commented, "Humph! He might as least wait until he was here long enough to get his feet warm before running for office."

Then why is it that the Granite State receives an inordinate amount of media attention for this quadrennial event? There are many explanations — some obvious, some subtle.

We have the distinct advantage of being the first primary stop on the road to the White House. The state is small enough so that any aspirant can compete with limited resources. Additionally our citizens and our economy are suffficiently diversified to qualify for good test patterns.

Perhaps inherited from our Blue Laws, which provided "common scolds shall be placed on the ducking-stool and wetted ten times," we take politics as a requisite civic responsibility.

There are a few critics among us who say it's good to have four years between presidentials because it takes them that long to regain their faith in the government. Probably they don't vote anyway. Still, allowing they may have a point, we cannot minimize the economic therapy these elections provide.

Politics has gotten so expensive it even takes lots of money to get beaten. Meanwhile our restaurants, hotels and liquor stores are pocketing the travel stipends of the national media.

It's a wondrous situation where the candidates and the journalists put on the spectacle and then pay us for giving them the opportunity.

Of course we must be constantly on the alert lest those jealous of our crown in the electoral process steal away our coronation rights. California, for example, takes the position that candidates need not be plowing through snow here when they could be snowing its citizens under its comfortable March sun. They don't mention their own political "flakes" who have drifted here in past campaigns.

Some national motivators think we should join a regional primary. Forget it. Obviously, they've never read the small print on our number plates. We'll still be picking presidents in the next millennium.

1956: The Democratic Primary

Tennessee Senator Estes Kefauver won his second New Hampshire primary this year, with 85% of the Democratic vote. Kefauver was an energetic one-on-one handshaker, who often campaigned by dogsled. He had built a strong base in the state four years earlier, and his popularity here caused rival candidate Adlai Stevenson, the former Governor of Illinois, to ignore the primary altogether. Stevenson was actually the Democratic party's presidential frontrunner, and he eventually won the nomination. He selected Kefauver as his Vice-presidential running mate.

22

A ROAD TO THE WHITE HOUSE

It used to be said that anyone could grow up to be President provided they were at least 35 years old, native born, and had lived in the United States for a minimum of 14 years. It isn't that easy. The Secret Service won't admit you to the White House just because you say you want to be President. So, where do you start? You have to work your way to the Oval Office by beginning someplace. There aren't too many roads that will get you there.

You could file as an independent write-in candidate for President in the general elections of many states. If you won in enough of them to guarantee the votes of a majority of the electors of the Electoral college, you'd become President. Inasmuch as no one has ever won any single state's general election as a write-in candidate, this is hardly a practical path to follow.

The more traditional road would be to acquire the presidential nomination of one of the major political parties. First, you'd have to join such a party. Then you would have to win as the candidate of

---

Troubadour September, 1944

The storekeeper in one of the rural towns inquired of the wife of a man who had been reported as "ailing," how he was getting along. "He ain't hard sick," she replied, "but he's considerable poorly."

1956: The Republican Primary

President Dwight D. Eisenhower, still recovering from a major heart attack just six months earlier, ran unopposed in the Republican primary this year. But Eisenhower was known to favor replacing his first-term Vice President, Richard M. Nixon. Nixon's friends in New Hampshire, encouraged by Senator Styles Bridges, organized a successful write-in campaign for the Vice President. Nixon won 22,936 votes and a sure spot with Eisenhower on the GOP ticket that won a second term for the Republican nominees in November.

your party in enough states to guarantee a majority of delegates, pledged to you, to receive the party's nomination at its national convention.

Finally, your party would have to win the general election with you at its head. With all of these goals achieved, you'd be on your way to the Oval Office.

In the alternative you could skip all the party's primaries and caucuses. Instead you could go directly to its national Convention and receive enough votes there to secure the nomination. But this, too, would be difficult because most of the voting delegates would have committed to other candidates — at least on the first few ballots.

Another quick way to short-circuit the traditional lines to the presidency would be to gain the confidence of whoever did receive the party's nomination. Assuming the candidate named you as vice president, that you both made up the winning ticket at the general election, and that s/he later died or resigned the office of President, then you'd be the automatic replacement. Under these conditions,

no election of congressional approval would be required to confirm
your assuming the Office of President.

Once you've selected your party, the quickest, easiest, least
expensive and most effective place to start is in New Hampshire's
first-in-the-nation presidential primary. It has established a
tradition of being "Always First, Always Right." It has become the
one state which gets the greatest focus of national attention.
Moreover, its citizens are "politically friendly" to all candidates.

For a $1,000 fee and a pledge to be a Presidential candidate, or
even Vice Presidential candidate, for the party of your choice, you'll
be graciously welcomed by the Secretary of State to make a formal
filing. Or, if you prefer, you can even mail in your check and
"Declaration of Candidacy." If you don't want to spend the $1,000
to have your name printed on the ballot, you are permitted to
mount a "write-in" campaign for the office.

From the moment you file you may simultaneously become the
subject of local and national media attention. It offers a high degree
of free publicity which could not be purchased. New Hampshire
voters take their politics very seriously and are politically sophis-
ticated from their quadrennial experience of selecting presidents.
The state is small, making it easy to traverse and shake hands with

the citizens of all regions. It's a level playing field which allows the relatively unknown contestant the same opportunity as nationally recognized candidates to seek support for their campaigns. All are extended opportunities to speak before various citizen groups and to participate in political forums. The character and persona of a candidate can become as critical as her/his stands on the issues.

Every four years more men and women join the race for the presidency by starting from New Hampshire than from any other state. They come from widely diverse backgrounds and with a multitude of varying motives. Some like the notoriety, others expound a sincere message for the betterment of our country and there are those who only seek a ballot plaque to hang on a wall, confirming the honor of having been an entry in a presidential campaign.

New Hampshire's 2000 primary has started numerous candidates on the road to the White House. The odds are excellent that one of them will be sworn in as the President of the United States in January of the year 2001.

1960: The Democratic Primary

The day before this primary, Massachusetts Senator and candidate John F. Kennedy was the invited keynote speaker at a convocation hosted by the University of New Hampshire. Kennedy's only opponent on the ballot, Paul Fisher, was not invited. He came anyway, and delivered a twelve-minute anti-tax stump speech. Kennedy won by a landslide and went on to become President. Fisher, wealthy inventor of the pressurized pen used on all space flights, ran in two subsequent primaries but never did as well again.

PRESIDENTIAL PRIMARY TRADING CARDS

In 1998 the Library & Archives of New Hampshire's Political Tradition published Series 1 of the Presidential Primary Trading Cards. These attractive 3 1/4" x 2 1/2" cards are similar in design to the universally popular baseball cards. Informative and colorful, they bring to life the presidential candidates, and represent another first-in-the-nation achievement for the Political Library.

For Series 1, 48 previous New Hampshire presidential primary candidates were selected. Evenly divided between Republicans and Democrats, sixteen major and eight "fringe" candidates were chosen from each party.

A photo of each candidate, usually shown in color in an action shot taken in New Hampshire, appears on the front of the card. The back of the card records the candidate's date of birth, home state, years

Library & Archives of New Hampshire's Political Tradition

Richard M. Nixon

on the NH ballot and votes received, platform, statement of the issues, and a significant quotation from a speech.

The project was underwritten by a generous donation from a foundation established by former Governor Lane Dwinell. Governor Dwinell was an eminent New Hampshire statesman, having served successively as our Speaker of the House, President of the Senate, and Governor.

Richard M. Nixon
Born: 1913
Filed from: California

NH Primaries	Votes
1960	(R) 65,204
1964	(R) Write-in 15,587
1968	(R) 80,666
1972	(R) 79,239

Platform: Support for Eisenhower administration policies

In 1956 Eisenhower questioned retaining Nixon for re-election as Vice President. Nixon's NH friends engineered a draft write-in effort for him which resulted in 22,936 votes, thus assuring his position on the national ticket.

"It was a reassuring comment [the write-in] coming from the voters at a difficult time."

In memory of Governor and Mrs. Lane Dwinell

He was an ardent student of Granite State history, particularly as it pertained to politics, and had a great interest in improving public education.

State law requires that New Hampshire history be taught in the fourth grade. The mission of the trading cards project is to create an awareness and stimulate excitement among school children in the rich history of the state's political traditions, and particularly in the presidential primaries which have been held first-in-the-nation here since 1920.

The trading cards have been delivered free to every school in the state which offers fourth grade classes. Accompanying the cards is a study guide for teachers, to assist in their presentation of the cards to their students.

Additionally, the Dwinell Foundation has permitted the Political Library to fundraise by offering packets of the cards for public sale. Full uncut sheets, both framed and unframed, are also available. Political activists have found the framed copies to make handsome gifts and provocative wall decorations. It is anticipated that Series 2 will present those candidates whose names will appear on the ballot in 2000.

Purchase presidential primary trading cards by
contacting the Political Library.
Phone: 603-271-2081.
E-mail: questions@nhprimary.nhsl.nh.us

Note: samples on

★★★★★★★★★★★★★★★★★★★★★★★★★★★★★★★★★★

1960: The Republican Primary

Late in December, 1959, just before the New Hampshire primary filing period expired, New York Governor Nelson Rockefeller unexpectedly announced that he would not run. This left two-term Vice President Richard M. Nixon with no opposition on the Republican ballot. He received 89% of the vote; the remainder was divided among several write-in candidates. Nixon later fared poorly in the first nationally televised presidential candidate debates, and he lost the general election to John F. Kennedy.

THE NEW HAMPSHIRE "PLEDGE"

On December 9, 1998 New Hampshire initiated a pledge which will commit wannabee candidates for President of the United States to abide by its law, which provides for a seven-day window between the date of the New Hampshire presidential primary and a similar primary in any other state. Signing the pledge means they will not campaign in Delaware, which as of December 9th, had scheduled its primary to be held on the Saturday following New Hampshire's Tuesday election.

Since 1920, New Hampshire has had the privilege of holding the first-in-the-nation presidential primary. Except for 1996, when Delaware held its primary four days after ours, New Hampshire has also been granted the seven-day window.

If New Hampshire accepts reduction of the window, other states might move their dates up to one or two days behind the Granite State, which would totally deprive New Hampshire of its traditional effectiveness in the national electoral process. Seven days are needed to give the candidates time to reform prior to the following primaries. Candidates have to rethink their strategies, including fund raising, for the remaining primary races. The week also provides the media, particularly the weekend pundits, an opportunity to analyze the results, creating the "bounce" the winner gets from leading the field in New Hampshire.

Republican Congressman John Kasich of Ohio was the first to sign the new pledge. He was followed by Democratic Vice President

Al Gore. Before the week was out, Democratic House Leader Dick Gephardt and Senators Paul Wellstone (D-MN) and John Ashcroft (R-MO), along with former Senator Bill Bradley (D-NJ), had all signed.

The pledge was drafted by the New Hampshire Election Commission, chaired by Governor Jeanne Shaheen, with members: William Gardner, Secretary of State; Joseph Keefe, former Democratic State Chairman; and Hugh Gregg, former Republican Governor. It is endorsed by both the Demorcratic and Republican state party chairmen, and affirms:

"I am not currently a candidate for President of the United States. If I should decide to be a candidate, I (name of candidate) pledge I will support the first-in-the-nation status of the New Hampshire Primary, and that I will not campaign in or allow declarations of candidacy to be filed in any state or territory that holds its presidential primary earlier than 7 days following the New Hampshire primary."

Candidates can sign on at the Secretary of State's office in Concord.

Troubadour January, 1945

State House circles are getting a chuckle out of one advertisement appearing in the 1945 edition of the Brown Book, official social register of the incoming state legislature. A local firm of funeral directors is listed with other Concord business firms in greeting the new lawmakers. Their ad states: "Welcome to the members of the New Hampshire Legislature. We are glad you're here. Please call upon us for any service we can render you."

PRIMARY PROFILE:
MICHAEL LEVINSON

Aformer seaman, poet, author of the analogical *Book on Lev*, Michael Levinson traded in the red-and-black hunter jacket and coonskin cap he wore in the 1992 New Hampshire primary campaign for a brown straw hat, flowered scarf, shirt and tie in 1996. "Anytime you do a good deed, you put a nickel in God's bank. The president has the chance to create millions and this guy Bill Clinton is a dud," said Levinson. As a write-in candidate in other states, his slogan was: "If you can't be bothered writing my name on the ballot, then you don't deserve to have me."

Platform: He claimed that America's sagging economy could be revived by building 10,000 clipper ships to haul our exports all over the world and "we should let college students work on the ships for tuition." Powered by solar panels and wind, the vessels would save fossil fuels. Staffed by a few merchant marine professionals directing the crew of students, the clipper ships would be escorted by non-nuclear subs to prevent "old-fashioned piracy."

This (1996) was Levinson's fourth campaign for president and he had a carefully-planned strategy, pumping gas for customers at gas stations to make friends and distribute his position papers. Much of his energy in recent years was devoted to attacking television stations that denied him substantial chunks of free air time in 1992 to promote his candidacy. After the FCC refused to act on his complaints, he filed a lawsuit before the U.S. Supreme Court

> ## Troubadour April, 1942
>
> Driving along a back road last summer a car full of antique collectors were surprised to see on the porch of an old house a little old lady in a rocking chair that would be a prize in any antique shop. They stopped, asked for some unneeded road instructions and succeeded in getting invited inside. When about to leave an hour later they gently broached the subject of buying the rocker. "Oh, no," said the old lady, "I wouldn't think of selling it at any price. It has been in my family more than a hundred years. And besides, if I ever get lonely, all I have to do is to sit out on the porch in this chair and I always have plenty of company."

asking for the FCC to be declared unconstitutional.

In November of 1995, he wrote to the CEO of every major network in the U.S. and to New Hampshire's only statewide commercial television station, requesting that he deliver "a series of major substantive mass-media speeches on behalf of my campaign for party nomination and candidacy for the office of president of the United States, 1996," His objective was to win the election by securing free air time then, via the "live, unblinking camera, go one-on-one with the citizenry," offering his short and long term solutions to the country's problems.

He was featured on a CNN news spot in 1996 and mentioned in *Time* as one of the more colorful "fringe" candidates. Levinson considered himself "an attractive candidate with meaningful nonpartisan solutions to our prob limbs." "Politishinz" and "pallah tics" were his favorite avocations, when he was not promoting the poetic, "prophetic" synopsis of human civilization he presented in his 1971 publication. Once a creative writing instructor at the University of Buffalo, he still regarded inspiring young minds to be a major priority.

When Levinson appeared on Kevin Miller's radio talk show on Nashua's WMVU, he met an activist who had recently run for local office. Coming off a tough election fight of her own, she knew how it felt to be a political underdog. When Levinson said he needed a home base for the primary campaign, the former aldermanic candidate offered him her living room couch.

Levinson, a Republican from Buffalo, NY, received 43 votes in 1988, 44 in 1992, and 35 in 1996. Already planning to run in the year 2000, Michael says he'll do better.

1964: The Democratic Primary

After President John F. Kennedy was assassinated on November 22, 1963, Vice President Lyndon Baines Johnson assumed the presidency. Johnson, focused on a difficult transition for the country, refused to engage in partisan politics and so did not officially enter the New Hampshire primary. Local supporters organized a write-in campaign which won him 29,317 votes. A concurrent write-in campaign for Vice President resulted in over 25,000 votes for Robert Kennedy, but John Kennedy's brother and Attorney General never made it onto the national ticket.

THEY SAID IT ABOUT THE NEW HAMPSHIRE CAMPAIGN TRAIL

Senator Eugene McCarthy

> *"I think more people die in New Hampshire than win."*
> *"New Hampshire is like a suit of long underwear frozen stiff on a clothesline."*

Congressman Jack Kemp:

> *"New Hampshire is unique in the whole primary process. You are the winetasters for the whole system."*

House Speaker Tip O'Neill:

> *"New Hampshire is an odd-ball state."*

Peter Kaye, aide to President Gerald Ford:

> *"A hell of a state to walk in, because if you go forty miles outside a city, there's nothing but bears and trees."*

Jere Daniell, Professor of History at Dartmouth College:

> *"New Hampshire is not attracted to the 19th century. It's part of the 18th century."*

David Shribman, reporter for the Wall Street Journal:

> *"Little New Hampshire — devoutly conservative, fiercely independent, mischievously iconoclastic."*

Troubadour June 1931

Interesting personalities about whom human interest stories are told are still to be found in many communities. Their unconscious humor contributes to the fun of living. You may have heard of the New Hampshire justice who announced that he would hear only one side of the case. "If I listen to both of ye, how can I make a decision?" he asked.

New Hampshire Political Profile:
Daniell in the Lion's Den

Some said he had the oratorical skills of William Jennings Bryan, but Gene Daniell of Franklin would probably have preferred to be remembered as having the rhetorical talents of a Huey "Kingfish" Long. In fact, the populist Louisiana Governor once called Gene "the best street corner orator east of the Mississippi." It's a given that New Hampshire never had a better stump entertainer.

Gene's overriding vision was to redistribute the country's wealth and he thus became a disciple of both Huey Long and Father Coughlin. Always a man of action in achieving his objective, he was arrested and spent 30 days in jail for throwing stink bombs into a ventilator of the New York Stock Exchange. It was a successful assault on capitalism as no one was hurt and the market was closed for two days.

Subsequently, he was arrested in New York's Union Square for rioting, anarchy and disorderly conduct. He spent time in the Tombs Prison and Welfare Island. These experiences caused him to say, "I was forced to become a vacuum cleaner salesman in order to preserve my amateur standing as a politician and a criminal."

Gene attracted large crowds when he spoke outdoors. He frequently stood on top of his car with a mounted loud speaker. Forever hounding Public Service Company for its high electric rates, he relentlessly attacked the company president, Avery Schiller. He also frequently tangled with Bill Loeb, publisher of the *Manchester Union Leader*, whom he described as being on the "lunatic right." Daniell's best performances were when accompanied by and carrying on a conversation with his puppet, named "Low-ebb Diller."

As an attorney, the lather of his outrage with Schiller was further demonstrated when he had the PSC president on the witness stand. The examination went as follows. Daniell: "Pretty sloppy bookkeeping, Mr. Schiller." Schiller: (putting handkerchief to his head) "It's pretty sloppy sitting here in front of you." Daniell: "This questioning is a matter of great importance to the people. If it entails a bit of saliva being sprayed on you, then you, sir, must bear up as best you can."

Troubadour February, 1932

John Hay, Roosevelt's Secretary of State, had a summer place at Sunapee. He went there during the Russo-Japanese Peace Conference and left word with the ticket and freight agent, baggage man, and telegraph operator that all telegrams be sent up to his house immediately.

Three days passed without any messages having come to him and, becoming nervous, Mr. Hay drove to the station to inquire whether some messages hadn't come in. Thereupon the general factotum answered yes, that several had arrived but they didn't make any sense so he hadn't bothered to write them down or send any word about them.

The messages were all from the Department of State, and, naturally, were in code.

1964: The Republican Primary

Arizona Senator Barry Goldwater and New York Governor Nelson Rockefeller both campaigned heavily for a New Hampshire primary victory this year, but both were eventually outpolled by a phantom candidate who never filed and never came to the state. Henry Cabot Lodge was serving as U.S. Ambassador in South Vietnam when his son and other supporters mounted a successful write-in campaign on his behalf. Lodge led the Republican field with over 35% of the New Hampshire vote, but the party's moderate wing later lost the national nomination to Goldwater.

Philosophically a Democrat, he often ran as a Republican, serving seven times on the Franklin School Board, six times as the city's mayor, nine terms in the Legislature and one as a state senator. Gene also was a write-in candidate for the Executive Council, and ran for Governor and both chambers of Congress. He was a mover in the National Commoners, or Independent Party, and ran as its presidential candidate in 1932, garnering 600 write-in votes.

On retiring from the School Board he commented, "At times I've been a trouble-maker, but somebody has to be something that begins with 'B' in order to accomplish what is necessary." Later in life he told the press, "It was a terrible blow not to be a world figure or President, but I've learned to live with it."

Daniell served four years in the Field Artillery during World War II and attained the rank of lieutenant colonel. During the Vietnam War he encouraged his son not to register for the draft, which cost the boy a two-year prison sentence. He once ran an ad in Loeb's newspaper offering a $150 reward to any individual who could produce William Loeb "alive" on a public platform to debate the negative of the position: "There is no moral, military, or political justification for the war in Vietnam." The reward was never claimed. Daniell compared President Reagan to Hitler, and was recognized as the first public official to recommend the impeachment of President Nixon.

Before the general election but after Hugh Gregg was the Republican nominee for Governor in 1952, Daniell filed a claim in equity before the New Hampshire Supreme Court charging that Gregg had exceeded the legal limit for primary campaign expenditures by not fully reporting all expenses. Because of the urgency to have the ballots printed for the fall election, in an unprecedented action the court allowed the parties to appear before it for a hearing on the facts of the case.

Troubadour February, 1944

Sweetser's Tavern was always well patronized. On a certain occasion, when all had partaken freely at the bar, someone in the crowd offered to bet a stipulated sum with Henry Hunt that he could not lead his two-year-old colt up the stairs into the hall. Mr. Hunt, who was full of spirit, immediately accepted the bet and led the colt in triumph into the hall. The money was promptly paid, but a difficulty presented itself. The colt, which seemed willing to climb the stairs, utterly refused to descend, much to the discomfiture of its owner, who appealed to his neighbors to assist him, but in vain. They were inexorable until Mr. Hunt, in despair, offered to expend the whole amount of the bet in "toddy" with which to treat the crowd, whereupon he immediately received all needed assistance.

1968: The Democratic Primary

For the second time, incumbent President Lyndon Baines Johnson refused to file for the New Hampshire primary, and the party organized another write-in campaign for him. Minnesota Senator Eugene McCarthy did file this year, and campaigned actively against the Johnson administration's Vietnam policy. Although Johnson won the primary with 50% of the Democratic vote, McCarthy won an astounding 41%, and more delegates than the President. After this embarassing setback, Johnson chose not to run for reelection, and dropped out of the race.

Daniell was particularly concerned with a reception held by the Gregg campaign in the elegant main ballroom of the Wentworth Hotel in Newcastle, and an elephant used in a Keene parade. He thought the reported cost of the Wentworrth event was insufficient, and the use of the elephant had not been listed on the financial return.

Between the time he filed for the Supreme Court appearance and the date when the hearing began, Daniell took to the air on radio station WMUR and addressed the listening audience "to ask for your help and encouragement." He noted that Gregg reported the only refreshments served at the Wentworth reception were hot dogs and orange juice at a cost of $50, but he found that difficult to believe and assumed cocktails and hors d'oeuvres had been provided. He recounted that Gregg's receptions included three to four hundred guests and that he had an elephant in his parades.

Warming up to the subject Gene continued. "I think of my early days in high school when I studied Roman history. As Rome gradually decayed, the voting public were kept satisfied with bread

Troubadour November, 1947

Ernest Poole in The Great White Hills of New Hampshire credits the late Senator George H. Moses of New Hampshire with the following toast:

"The songbirds sing the sweetest - in New Hampshire
The flocks and kine are neatest - in New Hampshire
The thunder is the loudest -
The mountains are the grandest -
And politics the damndest - in New Hampshire!"

and circuses. Let's not start that sort of thing in New Hampshire. I suppose the Roman Senator who ended with his throat cut by the barbarians probably would have called Gregg a cheap skate. Bread and circuses are expensive."

The testimony before the court was hilarious. Jim Smith, the right and proper proprietor of the Wentworth, admitted the stately ballroom was "not particularly conducive to hot dogs." Thus, he had trouble answering the question of determining the cost for serving, "one person, one hot dog, not including the tip." Gene had neglected to include the charge for the mustard. Asked how many hot dogs were served, Smith testified, "I think they averaged about 3/4 of a hot dog apiece."

The elephant also came in for its share of humorous attention after it was disclosed that the animal was loaned as a gift by Benson's Wild Animal Farm in Hudson. Testimony was introduced that when the elephant came off the truck "his personality wasn't very stable and because of that he sort of got very rambunctious. He knocked over one of the sulkies." He also trampled a couple of gardens. The Gregg chairman commented, "They (Benson's) should have paid us."

The trial lasted for three days. The court rejected Daniell's claims and ruled that "any mistakes made with respect to reporting cannot be charged as 'willful violations of the election laws of this state.'" Gene's comment was, "With a candidate of the limited mentality of a Gregg it is difficult to prove intent." Fortunately for Gregg, Daniell had not raised that argument during the hearings.

Troubadour October, 1943

Ray Dore of Center Ossipee has brought in the best story heard to date as to why he should have some more gasoline for his outboard motor. He explained to the rationing board that his tank had developed a leak and had drained every drop.

"Just how did that tank come to leak?" inquired a stony-eyed member of the board.

"Now, I'll tell you the solemn truth. Truth is stranger than fiction. I was fishing for horn pout. I pulled in an old lunker. I pulled too hard and he went through the air and one of his horns hit that tank and punched a hole right into it. Awful light material in them tanks — yes, sir, awful light."

The board voted unanimously that Mr. Dore be advised to buy some grease for his oar locks.

WALK OF FAME

Paving the way to the Library & Archives of New Hampshire's Political Tradition will be the "Walk of Fame," memorializing the state's first-in-the-nation presidential primary. It will be built into the entrance walkway to the front door of the State Library. Blocks of the Granite State's renowned stone will form the approach, identifying the winners of each presidential primary election since 1952. Sculpted into each block will be the name, party and year of each candidate's victory.

Additionally, temporary red bricks will be laid for those candidates who have contemplated running in the year 2000. To qualify for such recognition, potential aspirants must make their consideration known to the Political Library before October 1, 1999. They will then be invited to participate in an on-site news conference to receive their personal brick, inscribed with name and party designation.

The expression of interest in entering the year 2000 race is in no way considered a commitment to file for the office. Even an individual merely toying with the idea of being on the ballot is still entitled to a red brick. After the election is held and the winners determined, all of the red bricks will be removed and replaced by granite blocks identifying only those actually elected in 2000.

This project was designed to accentuate the significance of New Hampshire's first-in-the-nation presidential primary, and to stimulate interest in the easy opportunity for any citizen to start here as the first step on the road to the White House.

WHY BOTHER WITH POLLING PLACES?

W e used to take pride in our right to vote. Using an hour or two on election day to go to the polls was a voluntary civic duty eagerly performed.

Times are changing. In January of 1996 Oregon elected a United States Senator by ballots which had been mailed to voters two weeks earlier. The state had no election day, no polling places and, perhaps fortunately, no exit polls for the media. Citizens marked their ballots leisurely at home, dropped them in the mail and thus fulfilled their civic duty.

Moreover the process resembled a lottery. Election officials, as the ballots were returned, consistently published current results of the voting much the same as gambling officials announce daily growth of jackpots.

Its sponsors said their system is less expensive than operating polling places and generates more ballots in any case. To Oregon's credit, however, county officials periodically posted lists of those who mailed in their ballots, thereby perhaps encouraging others to start licking stamps.

North Dakota also used mail-in ballots in the 1996 presidential primary. At least it partially preserved the tradition of an election day by not counting the mailed-in returns until election night.

Perhaps voting "made easy" has gone too far.

Think ahead. In this cyberage of politics, such simplification of voting is only the tip of the iceberg. Before long picking presidents may be even easier.

The voter sits in front of the TV, remote control in hand. A ballot comes up on the screen. Or, if there's no TV in the house, the voter could go to a public TV phone booth provided by the Federal Elections Commission.

The voter enters an ID number issued as a result of the Motor Voter Law — automatic when registering a car or visiting the local welfare office. The voter presses the button for the candidate of choice. Americans all over the world will do the same thing.

The vote will be instantaneously transferred through the internet via a satellite system controlled by the FEC to a giant computer at Election Control Center. The Center will probably be located at the home of a new bureaucracy in a new building in Washington.

At the termination of an authorized twelve-hour voting span, the computer will print out a tabulation of the worldwide vote.

A new President will have been elected.

Nobody will have had to go to the polls. Nobody have had to count ballots. More voters participated!

When this happens modern technology will have made politics purely a spectator sport — competing on television with football games.

The odds may be long on when this will occur, but don't bet that it won't!

Troubadour January, 1935

Some city folks visited one of the old farms, and seeing the old pump, asked for a drink of that nice clear, cold, sweet water, as only such a pump can supply. When their host supplied them from an old battered tin dipper, one fastidious lady said to the other one as the latter was about to quaff from the brimming beaker, "Aren't you afraid of germs?"

"What air them?" queried their host. The first lady explained germs as very tiny buglike creatures.

Said their host, his choler rising, "Lady, I want to say I've drunk from that well nigh onto sixty years now, man an' boy, an' my father before me, an' we ain't either of us ever seed one of them things yet!"

THE FIRST VOTERS:
HART'S LOCATION 1948-64

The New Hampshire primary first received national television coverage in 1948. It came from a small town in Crawford Notch in the White Mountains. At one minute past midnight on election day, the twelve registered voters of Hart's Location cast their ballots before the cameras, and a media tradition began. Hart's Location voters led off for the next three primary elections. Then in 1964 the television cameras moved even further up the road, when the honor of voting first in the nation shifted to the residents of Dixville Notch.

★★★

1968: The Republican Primary

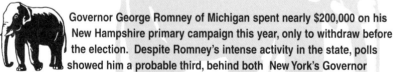

Governor George Romney of Michigan spent nearly $200,000 on his New Hampshire primary campaign this year, only to withdraw before the election. Despite Romney's intense activity in the state, polls showed him a probable third, behind both New York's Governor Nelson Rockefeller (a write-in candidate) and the politically rehabilitated former Vice President, Richard Nixon. Nixon won a decisive victory in New Hampshire this year, with over 80,000 votes. He went on from this primary triumph to win his first term as President.

PRIMARY PROFILE:
CAROLINE KILLEEN

A former Roman Catholic nun from Arizona, Caroline ran in that state against U.S. Senator Dennis DeConcini in 1982, and for Governor in 1994. An acre of hemp produces oxygen equivalent to four acres of most other plants which, she said, is good for the environment, and marijuana has medicinal benefits. It's time, she believes, to "bring hemp out of the closet."

Unmatched as a true grass roots campaigner, traveling always by bicycle, she pedaled across the United States at least ten times over the last thirty years. This taught her so much about America's demographics, being out there with Americans, that it became her lifestyle. She slept in fields, in churches, in college dormitories and homeless shelters, while "trying to look presidential."

"They used to call me a Bohemian years ago, a happy camper. But now, when you're out there in a sleeping bag and traveling, they call me homeless."

She had a hemp plant adorning her bumper sticker to tout the "re-legalization of marijuana." Though she pushed mainly environmental themes since her first presidential bid in 1976, the controversial candidate said she was anti-gay rights, calling her own lesbian tendencies "a curse" that she must sublimate "until there is a religious pronoucement on it."

Touting marijuana's medicinal and recreational benefits, she aimed her message at New Hampshire high school and college

students. She would lower the drinking age and promote smokers' rights. "Let Clinton inhale, legalize marijuana" was the bumper sticker she peddled statewide at $2 apiece, to finance her fifth bid for the Democratic presidential nod. She also used her Social Security check to help raise the $1,000 filing fee. "Willie's a wash and Perot's a horse's you-know-what," she said. "How could I not try again?"

In late January of 1996, during a record-breaking snowfall winter, our pro-cannabis candidate wore out her welcome at Phi Psi Panarchy, an undergraduate society residence at Dartmouth College in Hanover. House members were forced to call the police after several days of unsuccessful efforts to get Killeen to leave. One night of hospitality turned into two, then three. By then she had acquired a dog and became very upset when house members insisted she depart. Panarchy's experience is "not untypical of Caroline," said a person who knew her. "She does that quite a lot. She settles in and moves her stuff in and then doesn't want to move on." She did move on, finally, to a homeless shelter in Manchester, which became the headquarters for the final weeks of her campaign.

Killeen received 96 votes in 1992; 393 votes in 1996.

OPEN DOOR POLICY FOR VICE PRESIDENTS?

There's a 50% chance that a Vice President's foot is in the door of the Oval Office. Four of our last eight Vice Presidents, prior to Vice President Gore, eventually made it all the way into the room.

All four were subsequently elected to the Presidency (except Gerald Ford). During their terms as Vice President the country was lucky to have had such men just outside the door and ready to take over in the event anything had happened to the President.

We would not have been as fortunate if Vice President Agnew had taken over for President Nixon. This would have occurred if the Watergate scandal had taken place a little earlier. Agnew would not have been elected, rather he would have automatically succeeded to the position under the terms of the 25th Amendment to the Constitution.

This Amendment provides that: "In case of the removal of the President from office or of his death or resignation, the Vice President shall become President." It's an automatic succession from the Vice Presidency to the Presidency. No confirmation is required from any source.

Most inconsistently, the 25th Amendment further states that if there's a vacancy in the office of the Vice President, the President shall nominate a new Vice President who must be confirmed by both houses of Congress. After Vice President Agnew resigned, this procedure was used by President Nixon in selecting Gerald Ford as successor Vice President.

In recent years Vice Presidents have been the handpicked choice of the Presidential nominee and elected with him as a part of a political party's presidential package. The electorate plays no part in his selection. The Vice President makes it to the White House on just one vote — that of the Presidential nominee. And if the President becomes incapacitated, we get a replacement who was only subliminally endorsed by the people.

The irony of the situation is that we are more careful in picking supreme court justices, cabinet officers and even heads of many federal agencies than we are in replacing Presidents. All such appointments require ratification by the Senate. Should we not have at least as high a standard for qualifying Presidents as we do for Vice Presidents and other government officials?

The states are far more prudent in replacing their Governors. Most either call for new general elections or substitute someone previously elected to a subordinate office. In Vermont, for example, they have a Lieutenant Governor who is elected independently of the

1972: Democratic Primary

When the Union Leader published an editorial attack on his wife, Maine Senator Edmund S. Muskie allegedly cried at a public rally in front of the newspaper building. Muskie eventually won the Democratic primary with 46% of the vote, but his staff had publicly predicted at least 50% for this New Hampshire neighbor.

This made rival candidate George McGovern's 37% look like the real victory, and gave the South Dakota Senator a New Hampshire primary "bounce" all the way to the Democratic presidential nomination.

1972: The Republican Primary

Television comedian Pat Paulsen launched the first of his three presidential campaigns this year, with the slogan "The country cannot stand Pat." He came in fourth. California Congressman "Pete" McCloskey, who campaigned against U.S. involvement in Vietnam, managed 19.8% for second place.

President Richard M. Nixon, running for a second term, won the New Hampshire primary with over 67% of the Republican votes. Eighteen months later, he was forced to resign in disgrace amid the scandal of Watergate.

Governor. In 1991 when the Governor died, he was immediately replaced by a man who had already been endorsed by all of Vermont's voters.

In New Hampshire if the Governor is disabled during the first year of a two-year term, a new election is held. It it's in the second year, then the President of the Senate, previously chosen by fellow senators, takes over.

Even France has a better system than we do. It has no Vice President. Maybe we don't need a Vice President either. When President Pompidou died on April 2, 1974, general elections were held and a new President was elected on May 27th. If we didn't have a Vice President and didn't want to hold an election, a senior cabinet officer could fill the vacancy. Or the President, after the election, could name a Vice President to be confirmed by the Congress. Twice in the last thirty-five years our Presidents have been replaced. We've been lucky. In the future the suitability of a President's successor could be a gamble. We should close this half-open door to the Oval Office before an incompetent politician walks in to lead out country.

How About a Vice Presidential Primary?

It's logical, *why not?*

First, there's a need.

The 25th Amendment to the Constitution of the United States provides that if a vacancy occurs in the office of the President, the Vice President shall forthwith become President without confirmation from any source whatsoever.

But, if a vacancy occurs in the office of the Vice President, the President must nominate a successor Vice President who, in turn, must be confirmed by a majority of both houses of Congress.

Presumably, in the first case the Vice President is permitted to assume the presidency without confirmation because s/he was previously elected by the people. But, by tradition, the Vice President of the United States is selected by only one person, the presidential candidate, at the national convention of the particular political party. Thus, as a practical matter, though perhaps technically elected as part of a two-person "tag team," the people never had any part in the selection.

Candidates for the Supreme Court and the President's cabinet have to be confirmed by the Senate. Considering the awesome responsibilities of the presidency, a potential Vice President, somewhere along the road to the White House, should also be individually approved by the electorate or its representatives. There is a need to correct this deficiency in the election process.

Second, New Hampshire is uniquely qualified to fulfill that need.

New Hampshire is the only state where an aspirant can file directly for the office of Vice President.

In past elections such well known individuals as Wayne Green, a Peterborough publisher and businessman; David Duke, better known as the former National Imperial Wizard of the Klu Klux Klan; Endicott Peabody, former Governor of Massachusetts; and Senator Jesse Helms have paid the $1,000 filing fee to seek the office. Better yet, if a candidate is not sure which of the two offices is preferred; then, for an additional $1,000 the State offers the further option of filing for both of them at the same time.

Thus, New Hampshire has already set in place the procedure by which the voters can play a role in the selection of the Vice President.

This idea would encourage more voters to turn out at the polls. The Vice President under this plan might even end up being of a different party than the President. Then political activists could no longer complain about partisanship in the Oval Office.

WELCOME TO NEW HAMPSHIRE!

I n cooperation with the Manchester Airport Authority, the Political Library has inaugurated a kiosk at the airport. It is designed to inform the state's visitors about New Hampshire history, with special emphasis on our first-in-the-nation presidential primary. Located in the baggage pickup area near the auto rental and "welcome to New Hampshire" desks, tourists have ready access to the kiosk while standing to await delivery of their bags.

The exhibit is a "walk around" display which contains a video unit for the presentation of political tapes and/or documentary films relating to the state's history. Materials used are updated on a regular basis to assure continuing interest by the "frequent traveler." This showcase is a major attention-getter for the candidates, scholars, and media folk who visit us in connection with the year 2000 primary.

1976: The Democratic Primary

Virtually no one in New Hampshire had heard of Georgia Governor and peanut farmer Jimmy Carter when he began his primary campaign here. For a while, he was even known as "Jimmy Who?" But his traditional — and tireless — one-on-one style paid off. He came out on top of his better-known primary opponents, Senator Birch Bayh and Congressman Morris K. Udall, and went on to win both his party's nomination and the presidency, defeating incumbent President Gerald R. Ford in November.

NEW HAMPSHIRE POLITICAL PROFILES: THE ENDURING GUBERNATORIAL CANDIDATE

Many are the diehard gubernatorial candidates who've taken their defeats and risen to try again, but none with the consistency of "Old Buzz." Over three decades he tried and failed thirteen times, always further distinguishing himself by finishing last. Though a dedicated Republican, he once tried as a Democrat. Still no luck, though he agreed to quit the job after one year if the voters were "not satisfied with my way of bettering New Hampshire."

Running with the slogan, "Don't be funny, vote for Bussey," Elmer E. Bussey of Salem was perhaps the most intriguing character ever to appear on the Granite State political scene. He was somewhat handicapped by a virtually toothless face and a glass eye. He complained that New Hampshire needed more sensible employees on its payroll because, to qualify for a driving license, he was examined by an eye specialist and compelled to wear glasses to improve the vision of the glass eye.

A likeable gent, he'd served in the civil service under Presidents Hoover, Coolidge, Roosevelt and Truman before moving to Salem and working for 27 years as a faithful employee of Rockingham Race Track. Undoubtedly it was while working at the Track that he formed his views on state government and, more particularly, about the Legislature, as many of its members staffed the betting windows.

He alternately referred to them as either "lunkheads" or "pinheaded."

While hand-scything the hay around the Track at $1.70 an hour, busy Buzz had plenty of time to sharpen his opinions on state government. For example, he never liked the Highway Department because they couldn't "build a new piece of road without including a bad curve in it." He alleged that every city and town has the curve problem and "you don't have to drive a car very far to meet some nit-wit who likes to keep to the left when going around the curve."

After several years classified as a handyman, Bussey promoted himself to a "pulpwood businessman." In that capacity he vowed to clean the "deadwood" out of all the other state departments. Yet he was always solicitous of the Secretary of State's office where he was an incessant filer, and he delivered a bucket of smelt to give the Secretary "a good feed."

His campaigns were frugal and honest. At the time when Sherm Adams was in trouble with Bernard Goldfine over the vicuna coat, Buzz's return listed: "Expenditures, $27.40. Contributions none — plus nothing from Goldfine."

Because he capitalized on the word "Buzz" and consistently belittled state employees, one Governor suggested he consolidate his platform with the jingle: "The bee is such a busy soul, he has no time for birth control. And that is why in times like these, we have so many sons of bees."

Elmer kept buzzing without a reply.

Troubadour February, 1934

When nerves are jangling, walk with a dog through the woods or climb a mountain.

"FRONTLOADING" — A NEW TERM IN THE PRESIDENTIAL PRIMARY LEXICON

Since 1920 New Hampshire has rejoiced in throwing out the first ball at the opening of every presidential season. Though there has been occasional sparring over the privilege, until recent elections no other state had seriously contended for our February game. Iowa's earlier caucus never bothered us, anyway, because we've always been pleased to correct its misjudgments with our primary results.

Times are changing. We've done such a good job that jealousy is developing. Some other states have joined the play, detracting from our game. Super Tuesday was created. Florida followed us by a week. Delaware by only five days. California jumped from June to

---

Troubadour February, 1943

Joe Cram of Clinton Grove, Weare, was a Civil War veteran, an ardent fisherman and storyteller. One day a schoolteacher who was boarding at Joe's started to remove his rubbers. He put his left foot over his right knee, inserted his thumb behind the rubber and then suddenly fell into deep thought. A caller finally said to Joe: "Is he often taken that way?" "By Mighty," replied Joe," he sure is. I've known him to sit that way and stare and stare and he wouldn't wink no more than a knothole."

March. There's even talk of national regional primaries. Thus, the birth of "frontloading."

California is the 1,000-pound gorilla in this race. It's understandable that the good citizens of the Golden State, who constitute more than 10% of the nation's voters, desire more substantial impact on the selection process. In 1996, the presidential nominees were substantially predetermined before Californians went to the polls in June. It is for the same reason that Massachusetts, New York and many other larger states or groups of smaller states don't want to be left behind.

The ultimate objective of the experienced campaigner is to accumulate delegate votes, and California sends the most delegates to the national party conventions. It is an especially rich prize for any Republican contestant because it is a winner-take-all state for the successful GOP candidate. The geography and demographics are so vast and complex that the promotion of political candidates requires substantial expense for advertising and the services of public relations professionals. California politics are wholesale.

Fortunately, no state is currently protesting New Hampshire's 75-year tradition of being first. This means the less-renowned aspirants will not have to launch their campaigns in California or any of the other major states. The candidate's best opportunity is

---

Troubadour November, 1938

Samuel Morey of Orford obtained a patent for the application of steam to locomotion in 1795. He built a steamboat and ran it in the Connecticut River in 1790. Fulton's boat made its first trip in 1807.

still to start in this state, where it is inexpensive and easy to address voters. The political novice who graduates at the head of the class in our primary gets a free media "bounce" up with the big names before running against them again in the south and west.

But "frontloading" destroys the election process.

As other states, particularly the larger ones, shorten the election cycle, there is slim opportunity for the unfunded winner here to reorganize rapidly enough to be competitive in those races following in quick succession elsewhere. A week or two of delay offers little time for personal campaigning, identifying workers, raising money and developing sufficient resources to meet the already-entrenched competition of more experienced candidates. Thereafter, the glitz and gloss of expensive polling, professional political strategists and packaged television messages even more freely exert their pervasive influence on the choice of our president.

Thus, "frontloading" not only deprives the nation's voters of reasonable time to acquaint themselves with the candidates. More importantly, it can expel good candidates before their time.

Troubadour March, 1946

It is difficult for many people to understand the ruggedness of those brought up in the country districts and wooded sections of New Hampshire. I recently saw a photograph of Fred Scott, one of the game wardens in New Hampshire's north country, and a two hundred and fifty pound bear which he was holding. Fred said that when his friend was almost ready to snap the picture, the sun went under a cloud, and he had to hold the bear for two and one half hours until the sun came out again.

PRIMARY PROFILE
BILLIE JOE CLEGG

Billie claimed that he was ordained a minister on the streets of Exeter in 1976. He always carried a large-print Bible tucked under his left arm when seeking votes. Making his seventh try for the White House in 1996, having dedicated twenty years to quadrennial campaigning and accepting no donations, he guessed he had spent $10,000 of his own money. He saw the moral decline in our country back in 1972, and he had been running ever since. Though the national media completely ignored him, he said he was regarded as the most "colorful" candidate, sought after and interviewed by several radio stations across the country. 1996 was a great year for Billie Joe, as "only one out of every fifty people refused to take my pamphlet."

Platform: In order to boost the job base in northern New England, Clegg would establish a "state of the art" anti-missile defense base in New Hampshire. His plan called for balancing the federal budget within twenty years without hurting veterans, the elderly, Medicare and Medicaid.

Billie Joe took credit for having advocated a flat tax and preaching family values for twenty years. "Now, everybody's on the bandwagon." He'd replace the United Nations with a two-hundred-man SWAT team in each country.

Clegg wanted to "call out the National Guard and close down all the abortion clinics." He was opposed to the Federal Reserve, the

IRS, United Nations, affirmative action, homosexuality, and he would place a four-year moratorium on foreign aid and federal regulations. He was "for what God is for and against what God is against....By the way, what is all this I hear about our poor grandchildren's future?" he asked, reading from a written speech. "Let them stop getting pregnant, get rid of their sound boxes and earn a living like we did and our forefathers did. I read in the news the other day that the federal government spends $37 billion on teenage pregnancy. Maybe the parents should go back to medieval times and provide chastity belts for their daughters."

"It'll be a miracle if I become president, but miracles do happen. The reason I don't get elected is that I'm politically incorrect....I'm pretty blunt," he added.

He was a veteran of World War II, the Korean action, and Vietnam. He retired from the U.S. Air Force after serving twenty years, eight years overseas. He graduated from Oklahoma City University in 1978 at age 50, attaining a B average.

A switch hitter, Reverend Clegg received 174 votes as a Democrat in 1976, and as a Republican, 110 votes in 1992 and 118 votes in 1996. Sadly, he will not compete again as he died in 1997.

Record-holding Granddad
Plans to Revisit in 2000

In 1997 Harold Stassen, the 91-year-old "Grandfather" of the New Hampshire primary, granted an extensive interview to the Political Library about his experiences with the first-in-the-nation primary. The former Minnesota Governor (born April 13, 1907) had previously been on our ballot seven times, setting the all-time record for frequency of participation in the state's quadrennial event.

On October 17, 1998, in response to our question would he try again in the year 2000, Governor Stassen wrote:

> *"If I am blessed with good health in the year 2000,*
> *I will add another year!!"*

1976: The Republican Primary

California Governor Ronald W. Reagan made his first try for the presidency this year, and just barely missed the gold ring in the New Hampshire primary. His opponent, incumbent President Gerald E. Ford, never got much enthusiastic support from the party here. He was linked to national inflation and to his controversial pardon for disgraced ex-President Richard Nixon. Nevertheless, he managed to eke out a small triumph, winning the closest race in New Hampshire primary history by just 1,587 votes.

FIRST IN THE NATION:
A LEGACY

For over forty years New Hampshire's first-in-the-nation presidential primary has earned national prestige. Not generally known is the Republican heritage that makes it appropriate for the state to deserve this honor.

It all began when fourteen prestigious politicians met at Major Blake's Hotel in Exeter on October 12, 1853, at the call of former New Hampshire Congressman Amos Tuck. The group represented

---

Troubadour May, 1943

"Didn't see yer at Farmers' Night meeting," remarked one farmer to another he met on the street.

"Nope, didn't git to go," replied the other. "Good meetin'?"

"Pretty good of its kind."

"Vittles good?"

"Yes, everythin considered."

"How was the speakin"?"

Looking furtively over his shoulder, and lowering his voice, the farmer who attended the meeting confided: "To tell yer the truth, I'd most a felt I was wastin" my time if I hadn't of been settin' down."

the state's "top brass" of the anti-Democratic Whigs, Independent Democrats, Free Soil, and American Know-Nothing parties, all of whom were embittered toward the Democratic leadership. At that time New Hampshire had a Democratic governor and another New Hampshire Democrat, Franklin Pierce, was serving as President of the United States.

Amos Tuck suggested the name "Republican" for the new, emerging coalition which was "adopted by all who had acted in accord." The name was selected as an abstraction of the old party designation "Democratic-Republicans" first used by Thomas Jefferson and James Madison. Another New Hampshire resident, Horace Greeley, editor of the *New York Tribune*, was informed about the meeting and thus announced the name in the *Tribune*, giving it national publicity.

And so it was that the Republican Party was first named, formed, and nationally proclaimed by New Hampshire men from a meeting in Exeter, New Hampshire, held in the year before there were any Republican stirrings elsewhere.

1980: The Democratic Primary

Incumbent President Jimmy Carter was challenged this year by California Governor Jerry Brown and Massachusetts Senator Edward Kennedy. President Carter had the support of the nation as he tried to resolve the unending Iran hostage crisis, but continuing high inflation and interest rates hurt him politically. Kennedy came within 10% of winning the New Hampshire primary, and he didn't withdraw from the race until the Democratic National Convention had already begun. Jimmy Carter won his party's nomination once again, but lost the Presidency to Ronald Reagan.

The Saga of the Republican Party's Birthplace
AMOS TUCK "FATHER' OF THE REPUBLICAN PARTY
Genealogical and Family History of the State of N.H.

Tuck called a meeting of Anti-Slavery men of all parties with a view to better co-operation and united action. The meeting was held, October 12, 1853, at Major Blake's hotel, later the Squamscott House, in Exeter, and on this occasion Mr. Tuck proposed the name Republican for the new party. The credit for the christening is usually given to Horace Greeley; but his suggestion was not made till the next year; and the great honor of the name belongs to Amos Tuck.

RIPON, WISCONSIN CLAIMS ORIGIN OF THE GOP

RIPON (*The Ripon Commonwealth Press*) 10/21/93: "Every few years some burg or another — usually east of the Mississippi River — lays claim to being the birthplace of the Republican Party.

Troubadour September, 1941
Letter from Nathaniel Hawthorne to his publishers:

"I sha'nt have the new story ready by November for I am never good for anything in the literary way till after the first autumnal frost, which has somewhat such an effect on my imagination that it does on the foliage about me - multiplying and brightening its hues."

Now comes forth Exeter, NH, a town of about 14,000 granite-faced citizens.

HEY, WHERE HAVE THOSE people been? Like 150 years of silence? C'mon! Are they just now waking up like Rip (or is it Ripon) Van Winkle and figuring out a new way to make a tourist buck? Is the profile and attraction of the Old Man of the Mountain on Profile Mountain wearing off? Is the prospect of another bone-chilling winter disconcerting? Is the fact that New Hampshire is squeezed between Vermont and Maine uncomfortable?

A Democrat in Washington named Amos Tuck was thinking about a new party. He was head of the New England tourist bureau and simply expressed his viewpoint at a public meeting. "I wish we could try something new," he was heard to exclaim. But his friends were not excited. Typically New Englandish, they said, "Why fix it if it ain't broke?" Tuck went out and drank heavily at the local tavern. That was it.

NEW HAMPSHIRE CAN claim Lake Winnipesaukee, the longest body of water with the longest name in America. And it can boast about providing Franklin Pierce, one of our more memorable

1980: The Republican Primary

California Governor Ronald Reagan roared back this year, rolling over his six opponents with nearly 50% of the Republican vote. A campaign turning point came shortly before the primary, at a debate between Reagan and George Bush sponsored by The Nashua Telegraph and funded by Reagan. When the newspaper closed the other five candidates out of the debate without a protest from Bush, Reagan took over, announcing "I paid for this microphone, Mr. Green!" Once again, the New Hampshire "primary bounce" saw a candidate well on his way to the White House.

presidents — in 1853. But, birthplace of the Republican Party, it cannot claim.

Besides, Exeter sounds utterly too British."

Encyclopedia Britannica Says Exeter is GOP's Birthplace

CONCORD (AP) 10/10/97: "Exeter—not Ripon, Wis.—is the official birthplace of the Republican Party, according to the newest edition of Britannica Online. The new text says,'The earliest meetings of people who may be identified as Republicans were held in October 1853 in Exeter, NH, and in May 1854 in Ripon, Wis.'"

Troubadour June, 1943

Walter Capron had a blacksmith shop a little southwest of the old meeting house where he plied his trade for a number of years. Whatever faults Mr. Capron may have possessed, he was evidently a man of his word. At one time he was sorely tried by a prominent citizen who took the liberty to tie his horse in the shop every Sabbath morning without leave. Mr. Capron was so incensed at this that he declared if the offense was repeated he would shoe the horse and collect pay for the same. On the following Sabbath, the horse was found in its accustomed place in the shop, and Mr. Capron, good as his word, immediately shod it all around; the noise of the anvil somewhat disturbing the good people who were listening to the ministrations of Rev. Halloway Fish. It is perhaps needless to add that the horse was ever afterwards found tied in the meeting house sheds by the side of those of his neighbors."

1984: The Democratic Primary

Colorado Senator Gary Hart emerged from a pack of better-known Democrats to win New Hampshire's Democratic primary this year. His opponents included John Glenn, Jesse Jackson, George McGovern, and Walter Mondale, the former Vice President and media-proclaimed national "frontrunner," who lost to Hart by 10 percentage points. Mondale subsequently scored with an anti-Hart campaign based on a fast food ad ("Where's the beef?"), and he eventually prevailed to win his party's nomination. But his unexpected loss in New Hampshire foreshadowed the coming general election defeat by Ronald Reagan.

FILING FOR OFFICE:
THE PRICE IS RIGHT

Any U.S. citizen who meets Constitutional requirements, belongs to a recognized political party, and can come up with $1,000 can file to run in the New Hampshire primary for President or Vice-President or — for $2,000 — both!

Some candidates have tried to circumvent this filing fee. Austin Burton (also known as Chief Burning Wood, a Delaware Indian) once mailed a four-foot length of snakeskin to the Secretary of State, but was not permitted to substitute wampum for cash.

1984: The Republican Primary

President Ronald W. Reagan was a shoe-in for an overwhelming Republican primary victory this year, winning close to 87% of the vote. The closest Republican finisher was perennial candidate Harold Stassen, with 2%. Interestingly, six of the top ten vote-getters in this Republican primary were Democrats! Write-in votes for Gary Hart, Walter Mondale, John Glenn, "Fritz" Hollings, Jesse Jackson, George McGovern, Alan Cranston and Reubin Askew accounted for over 10% of the total votes cast. This odd result may be explained by the fact that for the first time since the New Hampshire primary began, Democratic voters outnumbered Republicans at the polls.

FILING FOR OFFICE:
SIGN HERE!

Candidates sign up to run in the New Hampshire primary at a "repatriated" antique desk in the Secretary of State's office, upstairs at the State House in Concord. The birds-eye maple desk was originally commissioned by the State, and made by a local craftsman for the opening of the State House in 1819.

Some time later the desk was sold and left the state. Twenty years ago, the State repurchased the desk from a Delaware museum for $5,000 — over 300 times the original cost of $16.

Troubadour January, 1943

Fish and Game wardens were first chosen at Weare in 1881. The town voted to protect trout and other fish for three years. "In 1883 the wardens were instructed to carry out the fish and game laws to the letter; also to allow the removing of the pickerel from Duck Pond for the purpose of introducing German carp. But in 1884 the town passed the following unique vote: "Voted, That the fish and game warden be instructed to stay at home." There must have been some prosecution for we find that the town paid, in 1885, $11.94 for "counsel on fish cases."

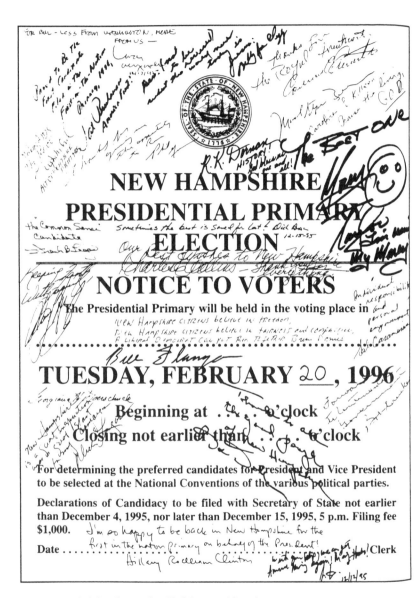

NEW HAMPSHIRE
PRESIDENTIAL PRIMARY
ELECTION
NOTICE TO VOTERS

The Presidential Primary will be held in the voting place in

TUESDAY, FEBRUARY 20, 1996

Beginning at . . . . . o'clock

Closing not earlier than . . . . o'clock

For determining the preferred candidates for President and Vice President to be selected at the National Conventions of the various political parties.

Declarations of Candidacy to be filed with Secretary of State not earlier than December 4, 1995, nor later than December 15, 1995, 5 p.m. Filing fee $1,000.

Date . . . . Clerk

Signatures left by those who filed for President in 1996.

74

THE Y2K NEW HAMPSHIRE PRIMARY: DATES, FILING, DELEGATES

New Hampshire law requires our primary be held "on the Tuesday at least seven days immediately preceding the date on which any other state shall hold a similar election, whichever is earlier." Consequently, the date of the 2000 presidential primary in New Hampshire will not be determined until all other states set their primary dates — probably in the early fall of 1999.

FILING IN 1999 FOR THE 2000 PRIMARY

Filing in 1999 for the 2000 New Hampshire presidential primary is accomplished at the Office of the Secretary of State at the State House in Concord. The filing period will extend from Monday, December 6 through Friday, December 17, 1999, except Saturday and Sunday, December 11 and 12, when the offfice will be closed.

1988: The Democratic Primary

Neighboring Massachusetts Governor Michael Dukakis led the field of press-styled "seven dwarfs" in the primary with 36.4% of the Democratic primary vote — just about the same percentage that George Bush garnered for the Republican victory this year. Locally, Dukakis opposed the Seabrook nuclear plant, which both won and lost him votes here. Nationally, he claimed credit for and campaigned on the strength of the so-called "Massachusetts Miracle." But that economic boom proved cyclical, and not strong enough to carry him to the White House.

1988: The Republican Primary

Two-term Vice President George H.W. Bush won his first presidential primary in New Hampshire this year. Other Republican contenders to fill the legendary shoes of Ronald Reagan included Senate Minority Leader Bob Dole in his second try for the White House, Congressman Jack Kemp, businessman and chemical fortune heir Pierre DuPont, conservative Christian televangelist Pat Robertson, and Reagan's former Secretary of State Alexander Haig. Bush went on from this victory to win both the Republican nomination and the general election. His New Hampshire primary campaign manager, Governor John Sununu, became President Bush's first Chief of Staff.

Daily hours will be from 8:00 am to 4:30 pm, except on the last day of the period when closing will be extended until 5:00 pm. Candidates can also file by mail, except on the last day, when they must file in person.

A candidate can file for the office of President or Vice President, or both. A $1,000 fee is charged for each filing, at the time of filing. The fee can be paid in cash or by personal check. Also, provisions are made for indigent persons, otherwise qualified to run but unable to pay the filing fee, to file upon fulfilling certain statutory requirements.

In addition to paying the fee(s), a candidate must sign a certificate declaring place of domicile, that s/he is a candidate for the office s/he selects, that s/he meets the qualifications for the office sought, and that s/he is a registered member of the party whose nomination s/he seeks.

Article II of the Constitution of the United States provides that no one may serve as President unless s/he is a citizen, is at least thirty-five years old, and has been a resident of the U.S. for at least fourteen years.

Write-ins Can Participate, Too

In 2000 only the Republican and Democratic parties will be permitted to have their party designations and symbols on the presidential primary ballot. The Natural Law Party, the Reform Party and the Libertarian Party (and any other parties) will not be permitted to participate with printed ballot recognition. They did not qualify because they did not secure sufficient votes in previous elections. By meeting certain requirements, however, such political groups can run primary write-in campaigns, and take part in the general election which follows on November 7, 2000.

Write-in candidates often show up as add-ons to the primary election ballot. Normally such candidates are not competitive with those who file formally and whose names are printed on the ballot. There is precedent, however, for a well-executed write-in campaign to carry the day.

Here are four successful examples: In 1964, Henry Cabot Lodge won the Republican presidential primary with 33,007 write-in votes. In 1956, Richard M. Nixon swept the Vice-presidential primary with 22,936 votes. Topping that, John F. Kennedy won the Vice-presidential primary in 1964, with 25,094 votes. And in 1972, Spiro T. Agnew won the Vice-presidential balloting with 45,524 votes.

Selection of Delegates to the National Conventions in 2000

The number of delegates and alternates allowed to each party is determined by the parties' respective national committees, with one alternate for each delegate.

Between December 6, 1999 and January 10, 2000, all presidential candidates must submit to the Secretary of State a list of those persons they wish to represent them as delegates and alternates to the national convention. Those named must, in turn, file with the Secretary a certificate which identifies their domicile and states that they are qualified voters and registered members of the same party as their candidate. They must also pledge to support their candidate at the convention for so long as s/he remains a candidate before the convention.

Any presidential candidate who gets 10% of all the votes cast on primary day will be entitled to a proportional distribution of delegates commensurate with the total votes cast. S/he will not be entitled to any delegates if s/he fails to get 10% of the vote.

After Secretary of State Bill Gardner determines the number of delegates won by each candidate, he will notify the candidates. Candidates will then select from the lists previously submitted to the Secretary their final choices for delegates and alternates, and so advise the Secretary for confirmation.

Troubadour March, 1941

One Sunday, a minister was preaching an eloquent sermon in the Methodist Church at the Center. Some of the faithful members, weary after the week's hard work fell asleep during the discourse. The speaker noticed the nodding heads, made a dramatic pause then shouted. "Fire! Fire!" One sleepy deacon, suddenly aroused from his dreams, obligingly inquired, "Where?" Immediately came the scathing reply, "In hell, where you are all headed for."

FIRST-TO-FILE:
QUADRENNIAL PERENNIALS

In recent primaries, two lesser-known "fringe" candidates have generated publicity for their campaigns by vying for first place in line on filing day.

In 1991, Michael Levinson travelled all night through a blizzard, only to lose to Billie Joe Clegg, who had slept on the State House steps. In 1995, Levinson camped at a back door, but Clegg beat him again when workers opened the front door first.

Clegg didn't file first, though. A reporter had earlier let in Pat Buchanan's stand-in, who already waited upstairs. Right behind them was Caroline Killeen who couldn't run quite as fast and was fourth to file in 1995.

1992: The Democratic Primary

This year, Arkansas Governor Bill Clinton became the first person to win the presidency without first winning the New Hampshire primary. Clinton's campaign ran into trouble when allegations of his frequent and long-term marital infidelity surfaced. Even without that, however, Massachusetts Senator Paul Tsongas already figured as a "favorite son" candidate in New Hampshire. Voters here liked our neighbor's position on the budget deficit, and his courage in the face of cancer. (He even did laps in the Concord YMCA pool to demonstrate his physical fitness.) Tsongas won the primary, but Clinton finished a strong second despite the negative media focus. He proclaimed himself the "Comeback Kid," and got a bounce from the New Hampshire primary, after all.

1992: The Republican Primary

Incumbent President George Bush ran into trouble this year because he broke his previous campaign pledge: "Read my lips. No new taxes." His only significant primary opponent was Patrick J. Buchanan, a conservative political pundit and former speechwriter for President Richard Nixon. Buchanan's campaign advertising focused on Bush's broken tax promise, and tax issues generally motivate and mobilise New Hampshire — as most other — voters. Although President Bush did win the election, this turned out to be the year of the second-place finish in both party primaries. "Pat" Buchanan won 36.5% of the Republican vote, thereby embarassing the Bush campaign and gaining instant credibility as a national candidate.

Once inside the Secretary of State's office, the three quadrennial perennial candidates faced the press.

As Levinson eagerly detailed his grand scheme for building clipper ships, Killeen interrupted, "C'mon, Mike, don't ruin it for the rest of us." She then confided to the media, "He's a little flaky."

Caroline then took over, expounding on her idea of legalizing marijuana, whereupon Clegg interrupted her, asking if she'd talked to Jesus about the plan. "Yes," she replied. "I've talked to him. Hemp is a creation of nature."

That answer led Clegg to remind her and the newsmen that Jesus Christ was in fact Billie's campaign manager, and HE would never approve of pot.

1996: The Democratic Primary

Incumbent President Bill Clinton ran virtually unopposed in the Democratic primary this year, although twenty hopefuls officially filed to contest his candidacy. Clinton swept all of them, as well as twenty-two Republican write-in candidates, with 83% of the vote. He outpolled his closest declared Democratic competitor, comedian Pat Paulsen, by a ratio of 76 to 1. This was actually Paulsen's third New Hampshire primary, and, sadly, his last. But it was his first campaign as a Democrat. When asked why he had decided to switch parties, he said, "I don't think the Republicans should have all the comedians in the race." He might have done better to stand Pat.

Troubadour August, 1944

On one occasion in town meeting there was considerable difficulty in choosing a representative. Phineas Farrar having held that office for several years in succession, it was deemed advisable by many of the leading citizens to choose someone else in his stead, but being divided in their opinions, they were for some time unable to make any choice among the several candidates. A warm discussion was taking place when the old Esquire entered the room. He accordingly rose and said in his own peculiar tone, "Mr. Moderator and gentlemen, let me give you a few words of advice — if you want a man to represent you in the General Court of this State, send Esquire Farrar by all means, for he has been so many times he knows the way and the necessary steps to be taken. If you wish to send a man to Canada, send Col. Joseph Frost, he has two or three sons living there, and would like to visit them. But if you want to send a man to hell send Hezekiah Hodgkins, for he will have to go sometime, and it is time he was there now."

T he procedure for counting ballots is initially the responsibility of the town and ward moderators. Disputes may thereafter be referred to the Secretary of State. Within five days after a primary election, any person of any party for whom a vote was cast can ask for a recount.

The fee for a presidential recount is $500. But, subject to other restrictions not detailed here, the complainant will usually have to pay the entire cost of the recount if s/he lost by more than 1% of the votes cast. On the other hand, if s/he wins by reason of the recount, then s/he is refunded all fees paid at the time of filing.

The Secretary of State and assistants conduct the recount. The candidates and their counsels and assistants have the right to participate in the recount and inspect the ballots.

If dissatisfied with the Secretary of State's ruling, a candidate can appeal to the three-member Ballot Law Commission for a hearing on the questions involved. In most ballot disputes the Commission has the final decision-making authority to settle the issues.

Troubadour October, 1944

The start of an old deed conveying property in Grafton County reads, "Beginning at a stick in a hole in the ice."

1996: The Republican Primary

This was meant to be Bob Dole's primary, but the former Senate Majority Leader's third try for the New Hampshire gold was derailed by fiery social conservative Patrick J. Buchanan, who won by just over 2,000 votes. Millionaire businessman and publishing heir Steve Forbes ran for the first time this year, advocating a flat tax and financing his campaign with (largely) his own money. He spent approximately $3 million here, probably as much as his principal competitors combined, and certainly a record for New Hampshire primary spending. It didn't buy happiness — at least, not for the candidate. He finished fourth.

For the first time ever an Alphabetical Listing of Everyone Who Has Ever Run in the First-in-the-Nation New Hampshire Presidential Primary 1952-1996

✪

Includes
name
primary year/s
party affiliation
vote count
D = Democratic L = Libertarian R = Republican
Winners =

* indicates write-in votes
(Omitted are others who did not formally file or were not written in.)

Agran, Larry
1992 D 331
1992 R 7 *

Alexander, Lamar
1996 R 47,148
1996 D 1,888 *
1996 L 82 *

Anderson, John B.
1980 R 14,458
1980 D 932 *

Arnold, Gary Richard
1984 R 252

Arnold, Stanley N.
1976 D 371

Ashbrook, John M.
1972 R 11,362
1972 D 27 *

Askew, Reubin O'Donovan
1984 D 1,025
1984 R 52 *

Averick, Nathan J.
1992 D 7

Babbitt, Bruce
1988 D 5,644
1988 R 100*

Bagley, Hugh G.
1984 D 24

Baker, Howard H.
1980 R 18,943
1980 D 317 *

Bayh, Birch
1976 D 12,510
1976 R 228 *

Beckman, Martin J.
1984 D 127
1984 R 5 *

Benns, George W.
1992 D 12

Bertasavage, Norm
1992 R 23
1992 D 6 *

Blessit, Arthur O.
1976 D 828

Bona, Frank J.
1976 D 135
1992 D 65
1992 R 1 *

Bosa, Richard P.
1992 R 349
1992 D 3 *
1996 R 216
1996 D 15 *

Bridges, Styles
1960 R 108 *

Brown, Edmund G. Jr.
1980 D 10,743
1980 R 157 *
1992 D 13,660
1992 R 773 *

Browne, Harry
1996 L 653
1996 D 1 *

Buchanan, Patrick J.
1992 R 65,109
1992 D 1,248 *
1996 R 56,874
1996 D 3,347 *
1996 L 176 *

Buchanan, Walter R.
1984 D 132
1984 R 1 *

Burke, Stephen
1992 D 39

Bush, George H. W.
1980 R 33,443
1980 D 415 *
1988 R 59,290
1988 D 724 *
1992 R 92,274
1992 D 1,433 *
1996 R 11 *
1996 R 3 *

Cahill, John Patrick
1992 D 83

Caplette, Raymond J.
1984 D 19

Carter, Jimmy
1976 D 23,373
1976 R 591 *
1980 D 52,692
1980 R 788 *

Carter, Willie Felix
1996 D 85

Casamassima, Sal
1996 D 45

Chimento, Carmen C.
1996 D 656
1996 L 1 *

Clegg, Billy Joe
1976 D 174
1992 R 110
1996 R 118

Clendenan, Roy J.
1984 D 20

Clinton, Bill
1992 D 41,542
1992 R 1,698 *
1996 D 76,797
1996 R 1,972 *
1996 L 65 *

Coll, Edward T.
1972 D 280
1972 R 2 *

Collins, Charles E.
1996 R 42
1996 D 5 *

Conley, Paul B.
1988 R 107
1992 R 115

Connally, John B.
1980 R 2,239
1980 D 18 *

Coy, Elmer W.
1968 R 73

Crane, Philip M.
1980 R 2,618
1980 D 61 *

Cranston, Alan M.
1984 D 2,136
1984 R 107

Crommelin, John G.
1968 D 186

Cuomo, Mario
1992 D 6,577 *
1992 R 799 *

Curtis, Dean Adams
1992 D 43

Daniels, Bruce C.
1996 D 312
1996 R 4 *

Dass, Michael E.
1996 D 57

Daugherty, Paul C.
1992 R 53

Dennerll, Norbert G. Jr.
1988 D 18

Deutsch, Barry J.
1992 D 26

Di Donato, Florenzo
1988 D 84

Doerschuck, Georgiana H.
1992 R 57
1996 R 154

Dole, Robert B.
1980 R 597
1980 D 3 *
1988 R 44,797
1988 D 591 *
1996 R 54, 738
1996 D 1,257 *
1996 L 67 *

Dornan, Robert K.
1996 D 21

Drucker, Robert F.
1988 R 83
1996 D 81

Ducey, Susan
1996 R 151

Dukakis, Michael
1988 D 44,112
1988 R 585 *

Duke, David E.
1988 D 264
1988 R 9 *

DuMont, Don
1968 R 39

DuPont, Pierre S.
1988 R 15,885
1988 D 164 *

DuPont, William J.
1988 D 1,349
1988 R 22 *

Eisenhower, Dwight D.
1952 R 46,661
1956 R 56,464

Erickson, Oscar Adolph
1992 R 16

Evans, William Jr.
1968 R 151

Fabish, Thomas S.
1992 R 25

Farley, James A.
1952 D 77 *

Fellure, Jack
1992 R 36

Fernandez, Ben
1984 R 202

Fisher, Paul C.
1960 D 6,853
1960 R 2,388 *
1968 R 374 *
1968 D 506 *
1992 D 82
1992 R 33 *

Flanagan, William James
1996 R 48

Forbes, Steve
1996 R 25,505
1996 D 1,294
1996 L 103 *

Ford, Gerald R.
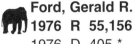
1976 R 55,156
1976 D 405 *

Fornwalt, Russell J.
1996 R 37

Fulani, Lenora B.
1992 D 402
1992 R 21 *

Gay, James Bryant Jr.
1992 D 28

Gephardt, Richard C.
1988 D 24,513
1988 R 180 *

Gingrich, Newt
1996 R 4 *
1996 D 1 *

Glenn, John
1984 D 12,088
1984 R 1,065 *

Goldwater, Barry M.
1964 R 20,692
1964 D 193 *

Gordon, Jacob J.
1968 D 77

Gore, Al
1988 D 8,400
1988 R 111 *
1996 D 679 *
1996 R 33 *
1996 L 4 *

Gramm, Phil
1996 R 752
1996 D 25 *
1996 L 1 *

Griffin, James D.
1996 D 307
1996 R 2 *

Gunderson, Ted
1996 D 70

Haig, Alexander
1988 R 481
1988 D 7 *

Hamm, Vincent S.
1996 D 72
1996 R 1 *

Harder, Heather Anne
1996 D 369
1996 R 2 *

Harkin, Tom
1992 D 17,063
1992 R 543 *

Harris, Fred
1976 D 8,863
1976 R 225 *

 Hart, Gary
1984 D 37,702
1984 R 3,968 *
1988 D 4,888
1988 R 91 *

Hartke, Vance
1972 D 2,417
1972 R 32 *

Hegger, Karl J.
1992 D 61

Higginbotham, Rufus T.
1992 D 31

Hollings, Ernest F.
1984 D 3,583
1984 R 697 *

Holmes, Gilbert H.
1992 D 39

Hoover, Herbert
1968 R 247

Horrigan, William Jr.
1988 R 76
1988 D 1 *
1992 D 53
1992 R 1 *

Humphrey, Hubert
1964 D 11 *
1972 D 348 *
1976 D 4,596 *

Hurd, John B.
1996 R 26
1996 D 1 *

Jackson, Henry M.
1972 D 197 *
1976 D 1,857 *

Jackson, Jesse L.
1984 D 5,311
1984 R 455 *
1988 D 9,615
1988 R 166

Johnson, F. Dean
1992 R 24

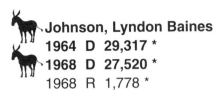

Johnson, Lyndon Baines
1964 D 29,317 *
1968 D 27,520 *
1968 R 1,778 *

Kay, Richard B.
1980 D 566
1980 R 2 *
1984 D 27
1984 R 1 *

Kefauver, Estes
1952 D 19,800
1956 D 21,701

Kelleher, Robert L.
1976 D 87

Kelly, David M.
1984 R 360

Kemp, Jack
1988 R 20,114
1988 D 233 *
1996 L 8 *

Kennedy, Edward
1972 D 954 *
1972 R 28 *
1980 D 41,745
1980 R 287 *

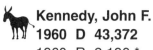 **Kennedy, John F.**
1960 D 43,372
1960 R 2,196 *

Kennedy, Robert
1964 D 487 *
1968 D 606 *

Kerrey, Bob
1992 D 18,584
1992 R 721 *

Keyes, Alan L.
1996 R 5,572
1996 D 281 *
1996 L 27

Killeen, Caroline P.
1992 D 94
1992 R 2 *
1996 D 391
1996 R 3 *
1996 L 1 *

King, William
1984 D 34
1988 D 36
1988 R 1 *

Kirk, Claude R. Jr.
1984 D 24
1988 D 25

Koczak, Stephen A.
1984 D 155
1988 D 47
1992 R 29

Kovic, Ron
1992 D 36
1992 R 1 *

Kreml, William P.
1984 D 25

LaRouche, Lyndon H.
1980 D 2,236
1980 R 19 *
1988 D 188
1988 R 7 *
1992 D 115
1992 R 17 *
1996 D 433
1996 R 1 *

Latchford, Vincent A.
1992 R 32

Laughlin, Tom
1992 D 3,251
1992 R 265 *

Lee, Richard E.
1968 D 170

Legas, Frank
1996 D 63

Lennane, James P.
1992 R 1,684
1992 D 6 *

LePage, Norman
1964 R 82

Levinson, Michael
1988 R 43
1992 R 44
1992 D 1 *
1996 R 35
1996 D 4 *

Lock, Stanley
1988 D 9

Lodge, Henry Cabot
1960 R 141 *
1964 R 33,007 *
1964 D 280 *

Loewenherz, Rick
1976 D 49

Lugar, Richard G.
1996 R 10,838
1996 D 410 *
1996 L 13 *

MacArthur, Douglas
1952 R 3,227 *
1952 D 151 *

McCarthy, Eugene
1968 D 23,263
1968 R 5,519 *
1992 D 211
1992 R 5 *

McCloskey, Paul M. Jr.
1972 R 23,190
1972 D 133 *

McCormack, Ellen
1976 D 1,007

McGovern, George
1972 D 33,007
1972 R 555 *
1984 D 5,217
1984 R 406 *

McManus, Gerald J.
1996 R 20

Mahoney, Patrick J. Jr.
1992 D 303
1992 R 10 *

Marra, William A.
1988 D 142
1988 R 6 *

Marrou, Andre
1992 R 99 *
1992 D 67 *

Martin-Trigona, Anthony R.
1988 D 61

Merwin, John David
1992 R 223
1992 D 3 *

Michael, Stephen
1996 D 94

Mills, Wilbur D.
1972 D 3,563 *
1972 R 645 *

Mondale, Walter F.
1984 D 18,173
1984 R 1,090

Monyek, Fanny Rose Zeidwerg
1992 D 29

 Muskie, Edmund S.
1972 D 41,235
1972 R 504 *

Nader, Ralph
1992 R 3,258 *
1992 D 3,054 *
1996 D 187 *
1996 R 94 *
1996 L 12 *

Nixon, Richard M.
1960 R 65,204
1960 D 164 *
1964 R 15,587 *
1964 D 232 *
1968 R 80,666
1968 D 2,532 *
1972 R 79,239
1972 D 854 *

North, Oliver
1996 R 2 *

Norton, Chris
1992 D 31
1992 R 1 *

O'Donnell, Edward T. Jr.
1984 D 74
1988 D 33
1992 D 24

Patty, Hubert David
1992 R 31
1996 R 17

Pauling, David
1996 D 74

Paulsen, Pat
1972 R 1,211
1972 D 19 *
1992 R 600
1992 D 2 *
1996 D 1,007
1996 R 8 *

Perot, Ross
1996 D 41 *
1996 R 24 *
1996 L 2 *

Powell, Colin
1996 R 649 *
1996 R 280 *
1996 L 43 *

Rackner, Mary Jane
1988 R 107

Reagan, Ronald W.
1968 R 362 *
1976 R 53,569
1976 D 875 *
1980 R 72,983
1980 D 1,958 *
1984 R 65,033
1984 D 5,058 *

Reber, Richard F.

1992 R 14

Rigazio, Donald John

1992 D 186
1992 R 10 *

Robertson, Pat

1988 R 14,775
1988 D 439 *

Rockefeller, Nelson

1960 R 2,745 *
1964 R 19,504
1964 D 109 *
1968 R 11,241 *
1968 D 249 *

Rogers, Tennie

1992 R 20

Romney, George

1968 R 1,743

Roy, Conrad W.

1988 D 122
1988 R 1 *

Rudnicki, Chester M.

1984 D 21

Ryden, Conrad A.
1992 R 20

Safran, John
1996 D 42

Sagan, Cyril E.
1984 D 20
1984 R 2 *
1988 D 33
1992 D 26

Sanford, Terry
1976 D 53

Schechter, Bernard B.
1976 D 173

Schiff, Irwin, A.
1996 L 336
1996 R 2 *
1996 D 1 *

Schneider, William R.
1952 R 230

Schwartz, Stephen H.
1992 D 17

Scranton, William
1964 R 105 *

Shiekman, Tom
1992 D 23

Shriver, R. Sargent
1976 D 6,743

Simon, Paul
1988 D 21,094

Skillen, Richard D.
1996 R 80
1996 D 5 *

Smith, Margaret Chase
1964 R 2,120

Spangler, Ronald W.
1996 D 62

Spector, Arlen
1996 R 10 *

Stassen, Harold E.
1952 R 6,574
1964 R 1,373
1968 R 429
1984 R 1,543
1988 R 130
1988 D 1 *
1992 R 206

Stevenson, Adlai
1952 D 40 *
1956 D 3,806 *
1960 D 168 *
1964 D 16 *

Stone, Willis
1968 R 527

Symington, Stuart
1960 D 183 *

Taft, Robert A.
1952 R 35,838

Taylor, Morry
1996 R 2,944
1996 D 167 *
1996 L 19 *

Thomas, Frank L.
1988 D 28

Thornton, Curly
1992 D 125
1992 R 6 *

Thorpe, Osie
1988 D 16
1996 D 50

Tomeo, Ben J.
1996 D 47

Trinsey, Jack
1992 R 22

Truman, Harry S.
1952 D 15,927

Tsongas, Paul E.
1992 D 55,666
1992 R 3,676 *

Udall, Morris K.
1976 D 18,710
1972 R 421 *

Van Petten, A.A.
1988 D 10

Wallace George C.
1968 D 201 *
1972 D 175 *
1972 R 93 *
1976 D 1,061 *

Watumull, David
1968 R 161

Weld, William
1992 R 51 *

Wilder, L. Douglas
1992 D 103
1992 R 30 *

Willis, Gerald
1984 D 50
1984 R 1 *

Woods, Charles
1992 D 2,862
1992 R 284 *

Yorty, Sam
1972 D 5,401
1972 R 55 *

Zimmerman, George A.
1992 R 31

Zuber, Paul B.
1964 D 2 *

Zucker, Irwin
1988 D 22

Troubadour March, 1950

A stone in an old cemetery in New Hampton
has the following epitaph:

UNDER THIS SOD HENRY ROBINSON LIES,
HIS MOUTH AND HIS GRAVE ARE BOTH OF A SIZE.
HUSH, READER, STEP LIGHTLY UP THIS SOD,
FOR IF HE GAPS, YOU'RE GONE TO GOD."